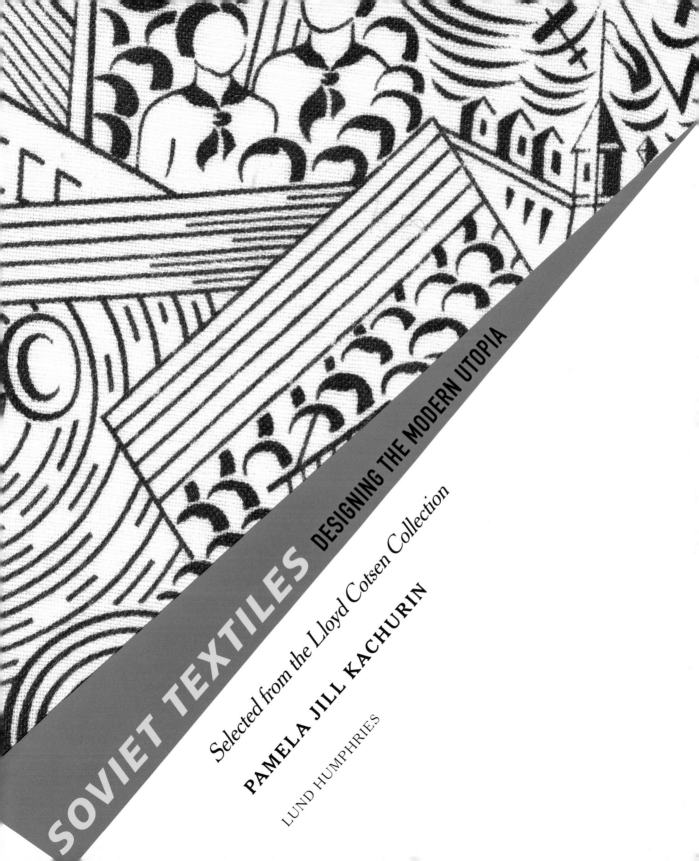

SOVIET TEXTILES

DESIGNING THE MODERN UTOPIA

Selected from the Lloyd Cotsen Collection

PAMELA JILL KACHURIN

LUND HUMPHRIES

Published in 2006 by

Lund Humphries
Gower House
Croft Road
Aldershot
Hampshire GU11 3HR
United Kingdom

www.lundhumphries.com

Lund Humphries is part of Ashgate Publishing

Published by arrangement with MFA Publications, a
division of the Museum of Fine Arts, Boston.

© 2006 by Museum of Fine Arts, Boston

British Library Cataloguing-in-Publication Data
A catalogue record for this book is available from the
British Library

ISBN: 0 85331 952 9
ISBN-13: 978 0 85331 952 8

Cover: Locomotives, 1920–30, designed by Sergei
Burylin, and Flag-waving figures, 1933, designed by
Darya Preobrazhenskaya

All works except for the comparative figure illustrations
are from the Lloyd Cotsen Collection.

All photographs of works in the Lloyd Cotsen Collection
are courtesy Museum of Fine Arts, Boston. © 2006
Lloyd Cotsen

Edited by Sarah McGaughey Tremblay
Produced by Theresa McAweeney
Photography by Damon Beale
Designed by Misha Beletsky
Printed and bound at Graphicom, Verona, Italy

FIRST EDITION
Printed in Italy
This book was printed on acid-free paper.

CONTENTS

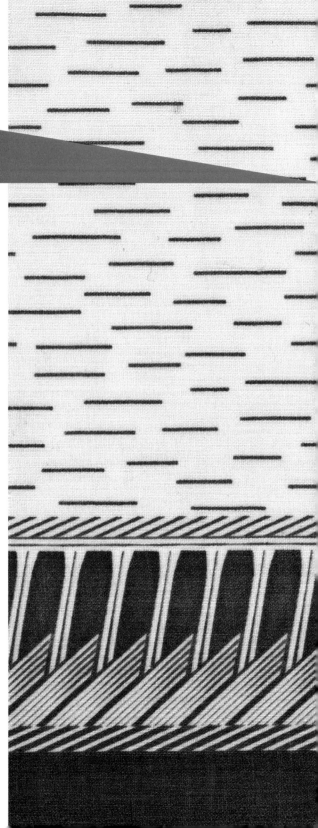

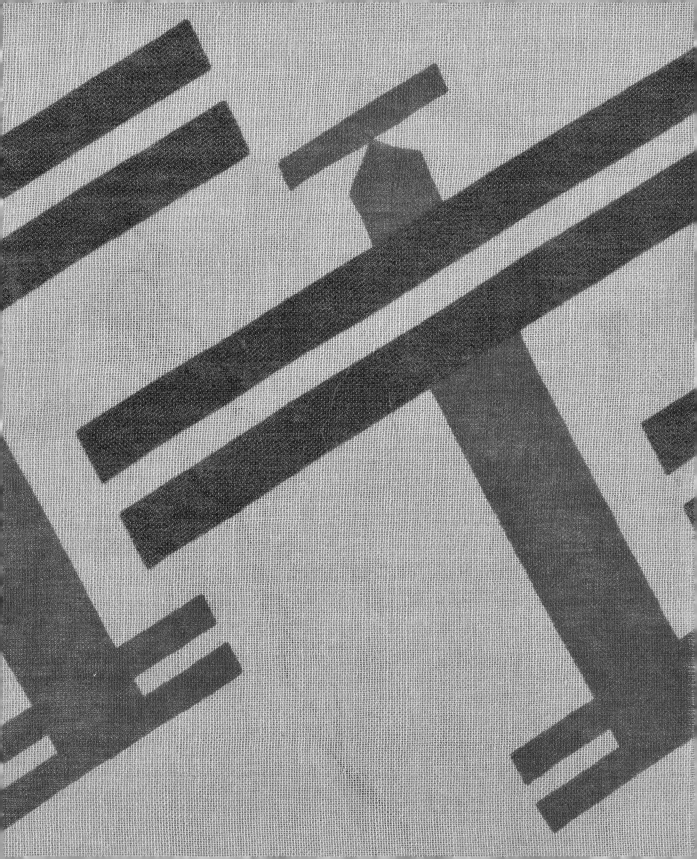

DIRECTOR'S FOREWORD

It is with great thanks to Lloyd Cotsen that we present his collection of Soviet textiles and drawings in this book and in the exhibition it accompanies. Mr. Cotsen has long been an avid collector of folk art and textiles, and he is deeply committed to sharing his treasures with a broad public. He is particularly interested in art that is intimately connected to people—to our desire to change and shape human life through the power of art and design. The works in this collection testify to his recognition of that desire.

Dating from the early years of the Soviet Union (specifically between 1927 and 1933), these textiles and drawings represent a period when the new Communist leadership was attempting to convert the predominantly agricultural nation into a modern, mechanized utopia. Some artists believed that mass-produced fabrics depicting such symbols of modernity as airplanes and electrical pylons could mold the outlook and actions of the masses to align with the modern Soviet ideal. The objects illustrated here comprise only a small portion of Mr. Cotsen's collection of Soviet-era textiles, but they represent the prevalent motifs that featured in this intriguing and short-lived experiment.

I am grateful to Mr. Cotsen, his curators Mary Hunt Kahlenberg and Lyssa Stapleton, and the rest of his curatorial staff for sharing his collection with us and making this exhibition and publication possible. I also extend my gratitude to Pamela Kachurin, author of the essay and guest curator of the exhibition, whose expertise in Soviet history has brought these works into focus for an English-speaking audience, and to Alexandra Bennett Huff, Curatorial Planning and Project Manager, for so ably overseeing the project. Finally, I thank Pamela Parmal, David and Roberta Logie Curator of

Textile and Fashion Arts, and her staff here at the MFA for their ongoing creative promotion of the significant and fascinating ways that textiles have been and continue to be an integral part of our artistic heritage.

> Malcolm Rogers
> Ann and Graham Gund Director
> Museum of Fine Arts, Boston

DESIGNING THE MODERN UTOPIA

PAMELA JILL KACHURIN

The 1920s and 1930s were a period of rapid industrialization, collectivization, and cultural revolution in the nascent Soviet Union. In March 1917, succumbing to political pressures, Tsar Nicholas II had abdicated the Russian throne and a provisional government had been installed. Meanwhile, the Bolshevik Party, led by Vladimir Ulianov (who would change his last name to Lenin), had gained popular support with its platform of ending Russian involvement in World War I and promising bread and land to the impoverished citizens of Russia. In October 1917, in a bloodless coup d'état, the Bolsheviks took control of the central government functions, and Lenin became the leader of the new Soviet Russia. The civil war that ensued from 1918 to 1920 ended with Bolshevik victory and the subsequent founding in 1922 of the Soviet Union, an officially socialist state under the Communist Party.

Every aspect of public and private life was touched by the Bolsheviks' campaign to transform the new Soviet Union from a backward, agrarian country into a modern, industrialized state. Central to this effort was the overthrowing of Russia's exploitative capitalists, with the hope that dismantling the bourgeoisie as a class and handing over control of enterprise to the workers would end the dramatic disparities that characterized the Russian economy. The Communist leadership was highly dependent on visual media to communicate these tenets to the mostly illiterate Russian population. During the civil war, it charged printing presses with the task of designing visually emphatic broadsides, such as Vladimir Kozlinsky's "Holiday finery: Then and now" poster, that could be easily understood and quickly digested.

As the textiles and drawings in this book demonstrate, even textile design was harnessed

Fig. 1

"Holiday finery: Then and now,"

poster by Vladimir Kozlinsky, 1920–21.

© 2006 State Russian Museum, St. Petersburg

РОССИЙСКАЯ СОЦИАЛИСТИЧЕСКАЯ ФЕДЕРАТИВНАЯ   СОВЕТСКАЯ РЕСПУБЛИКА

Р.Ф.С.Р.

ОРУЖИЕМ МЫ ДОБИЛИ ВРАГА
ТРУДОМ МЫ ДОБУДЕМ ХЛЕБ
ВСЕ ЗА РАБОТУ, ТОВАРИЩИ!

Fig. 2

"We have defeated our enemies with weapons, we shall
make our daily bread with work. Everybody to work,
comrades!" poster by Nikolai Kogut, 1920

in the struggle to modernize the state. In 1928,
a small but influential group of artists began to
promote the use of thematic designs on textiles.
They believed that printing tractors, smokestacks, and other modern motifs on clothing and
on household fabrics such as pillowcases and
curtains would not only have an educational
value—by presenting the goals of the new
state—but would also raise the wearer's political consciousness and assist in the transformation of that individual into the ideal Soviet
person. This person, by internalizing Communist credos, would be a reliable supporter—both
in word and in deed—of the policies laid out by
the Communist Party. In this uniquely Soviet experiment in social and sartorial engineering,
workers and peasants—simply by putting on
their shirts or skirts—potentially became walk-
ing billboards for the revolutionary initiatives
being enacted by the first socialist government.

The designs illustrated throughout this book
are textile samples and drawings from the major
mills in the Soviet Union. They date from 1927
to 1933—a brief period of experimentation—

and few of them were actually mass-produced. While some of the drawings are abstract geometric patterns, most of the designs illustrate a select group of themes that formed the core of Soviet visual propaganda during this period: the glorification of industry, the celebration of agricultural pursuits, and the promise of youth. The imagery employed in both the drawings and the printed textiles had been used by artists since 1917 to proclaim Bolshevik ideologies and programs, and therefore was immediately recognizable to the average citizen who had been immersed in Soviet visual language for more than a decade. Nikolai Kogut's 1920 poster, for example, is replete with popular images in the Soviet visual lexicon, all of which appear in the later fabric designs: male and female workers, hammer and sickle, smokestacks and factories, a Red Army cap, laborers repairing locomotives, electricity poles, and cranes.

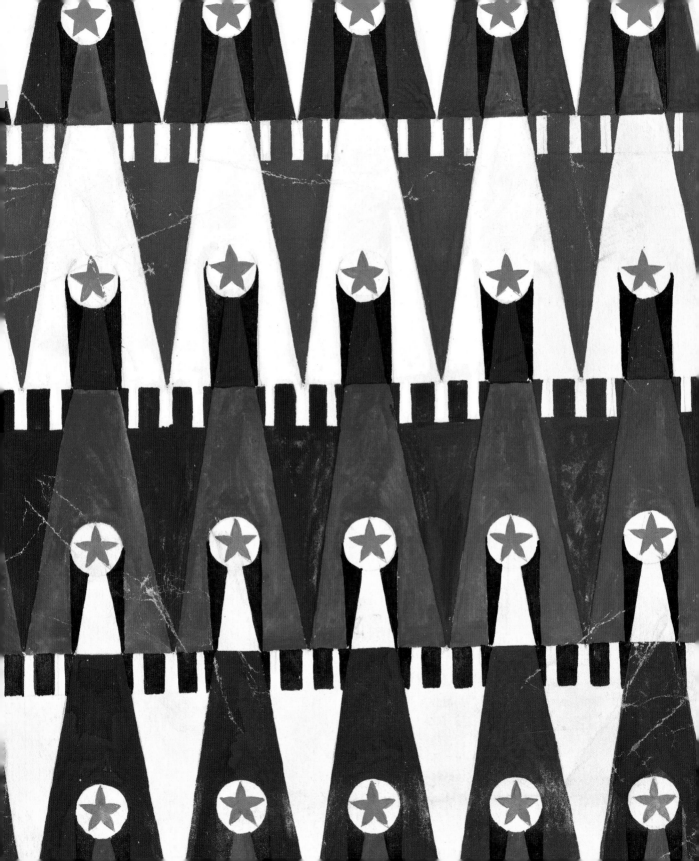

THE EVOLUTION
OF TEXTILE DESIGN

During the nineteenth and early twentieth centuries, Russian textile manufacturing had been a vibrant industry. Textile designers relied on European pattern books as sources for designs. Common motifs on textiles aimed at the growing urban middle class included exotic animals and birds, and historical subjects such as the War of 1812. Floral patterns were widespread on fabrics made for other classes, the majority of whom still lived in the countryside. While some textile and clothing production took place in small workshops, several large textile mills operated in the cities, including the Prokhorovskii Trekhgornaya plant, which was founded in Moscow by the Prokhorovskii family in 1799 and continues to operate today under the name Trekhgornaya Manufacturing.

One of Lenin's first acts as the new Soviet leader was to nationalize all manufacturing enterprises. By June 1918, only eight months after the Bolshevik Revolution, the largest textile

OPPOSITE

Stars and triangles, about 1930

Sergei Burylin (1876–1942)

Designed for Ivanovo-Voznesensk factories

Watercolor on paper

30.5 × 31.8 cm (12 × 12½ in.)

mills in Moscow, Petrograd, and Ivanovo-Voznesensk were nationalized, and their ownership shifted from private industrialists to the workers themselves. Many industrialists fled the country in fear of persecution. Others stayed and became managers of the factories they once owned. After the political and economic chaos of the civil war, textile manufacturing was one of the first industries to be revived, although on a very primitive level: in 1922 and 1923, most textiles were manufactured without any designs at all. This revival can be attributed to the Bolsheviks' commitment to the rapid industrialization of the entire country, which would reach its apogee under Lenin's successor, Joseph Stalin, who became head of the Communist Party in 1924.

Responding to a public appeal to help revitalize textile design, artists associated with Russian Constructivism, including Varvara Stepanova and Liubov Popova, went to work in the First Factory of Printed Cotton in Moscow. They were among the many Russian artists who chose to remain in Soviet Russia and work for the state, now the sole arts patron and employer. Their factory positions gave them the opportunity to assist in the building of the socialist country, as well as to earn a regular income and secure housing—rare commodities during this period of economic upheaval. As the heads of the design studio, Stepanova and Popova promoted a new type of textile design: rather than floral or European-based patterns, which were associated with the prerevolutionary bourgeoisie, their designs were entirely geometric, without reference to recognizable objects.

Stepanova and Popova believed, rather idealistically, that purely geometric designs were most appropriate for the emerging egalitarian and classless society, since these designs were without particular class associations. They made new types of clothes befitting the activities in which the new Soviet person would engage, such as labor and sports. The ideal person was physically healthy, vigorous, and energetic, and participated in sport as a form of communal activity. Stepanova, in particular, designed clothing according to the principles of comfort and functionality. Her sports uniforms, for example, were intended to be easy to put on and comfortable to wear, and displayed colors that readily distinguished different teams.

With the revival of the textile industry, the All-Union Textile Syndicate was created in 1922 to address major issues facing textile manufacturing in the Soviet Union, including the importation of raw materials (cotton and wool) to increase production, and the export of printed fabrics to China, Persia, Afghanistan, and Central Asian countries. The syndicate was the central organ that controlled all aspects of textile production, and the major factories (including those at Ivanovo-Voznesensk and Trekhgornaya Manufacturing, the plants where most of the designs in this book were created) were subject to the decisions made by the syndicate. The syndicate's Artistic Council exercised authority over textile design across the country, and each factory's design department included representatives of the council, who approved or declined the designs that artists submitted. In contrast to Popova's and Stepanova's classless geometric

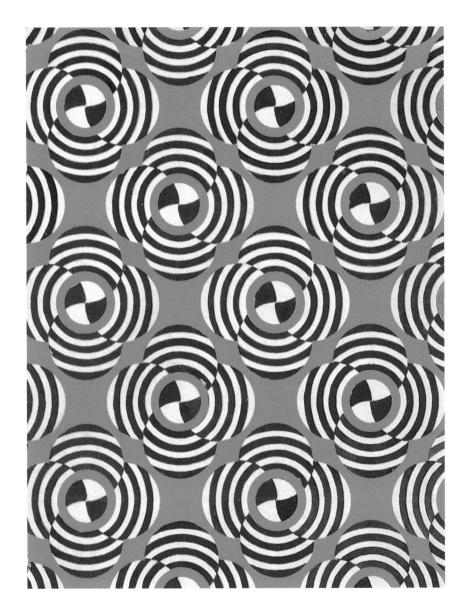

Fig. 3

Textile design by Varvara Stepanova (1894–1958),

1924. © Estate of Varvara Stepanova /

RAO, Moscow / VAGA, New York

Fig. 4

Design for sport clothing

by Varvara Stepanova (1894–1958), 1924.

© Estate of Varvara Stepanova /

RAO, Moscow / VAGA, New York

designs, the younger artists who dominated the Artistic Council were committed to producing a specifically Soviet textile design that would be connected with the Soviet visual language that had developed since the revolution. Recent graduates of the Textile Department at Moscow's Higher Technical Institute, these young artists firmly believed that thematic designs on clothing, curtains, and bed sheets could play a major role in refashioning people into model Soviet citizens.

Between 1928 and 1933, the debate over an appropriately Soviet textile design took place in exhibitions and conferences and dominated the pages of the All-Union Textile Syndicate's multiple journals and trade newspapers, which were aimed primarily at those working within the industry. In the catalogue for the 1928 exhibition "Soviet Textiles for Daily Life" at the Higher Technical Institute, the well-respected art historian and administrator Aleksei Fedorov-Davydov wrote that fabrics were "ideological goods" that could reach the farthest corners of the Soviet Union and therefore could have

enormous impact. However, in a 1931 speech reprinted in the trade journal *Textiles' Voice*, David Arkin, a scholar from the Academy of Artistic Sciences in Moscow, protested the use of thematic design on textiles, suggesting that they would lose their impact after a short time. The artist Lya Raiser took an extreme position, contending that *all* decorative ornament was bourgeois and therefore none belonged in Soviet textile design. Raiser advocated the use, instead, of simple slogans and initials such as "VKP(B)," the initials of the All-Union Communist Party (Bolshevik). The fact that textile design was a subject of debate during this time of dramatic upheaval reveals the substantial responsibility that was placed on visual images in this process of massive social transformation.

Although there was considerable dissent on the issue of thematic textile design, ultimately those artists who supported thematic motifs prevailed. They had maneuvered themselves into a position of authority in the textile world by attaching themselves to the influential realist art group the Association of Artists of

Hammers and sickles, about 1930

Sergei Burylin (1876–1942)

Designed for Ivanovo-Voznesensk factories

Watercolor on paper

20 × 14.3 cm (7⅞ × 5⅝ in.)

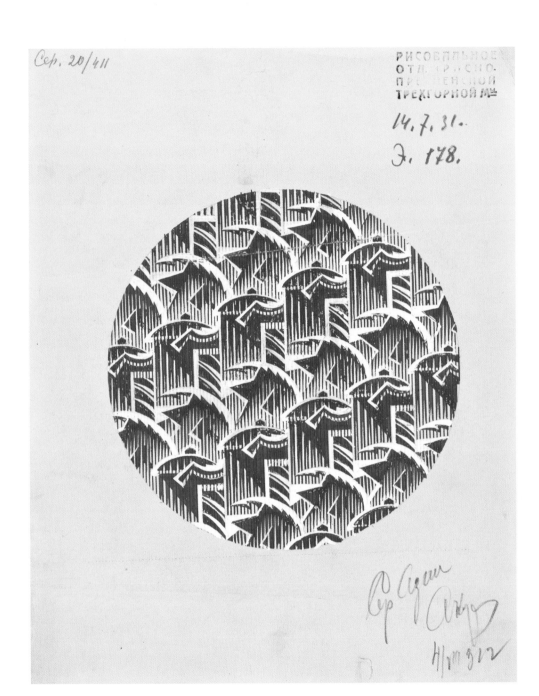

Soviet symbols, 1931

Designed for Trekhgornaya Manufacturing

Watercolor on paper

30.5 × 23.8 cm (12 × 9⅜ in.)

Revolutionary Russia. As the dominant members of the Artistic Council within the All-Union Textile Syndicate, they became the arbiters of which designs would be accepted for production. The Artistic Council accepted or rejected designs on the basis of both political and aesthetic merit. Often the council members would make suggestions about how to improve a particular design, but sometimes they simply rejected it for no obvious reason. Once a design was approved, it could be printed on textiles for garments or household use.

In addition to setting the standards for new designs, the Artistic Council conducted a thorough purge of factory design studios between 1929 and 1931, during which it destroyed about twenty-four thousand existing drawings and designs, most of them floral. By 1929, the council routinely rejected nonrepresentational or purely geometric designs in favor of thematic images. The themes were not mandated by the Communist Party or government officials; rather, the artists themselves devised them in response to major initiatives being planned and

enacted across the country, and the related propaganda. Certain initials, slogans, and symbols
were ubiquitous in the Soviet visual landscape
and were immediately recognized and understood as shorthand for programs and plans
sponsored by the Soviet government. The hammer and sickle, for instance, adopted as the
symbol of the Soviet state in 1918, incorporated
imagery of industry and agriculture in one in-
stantly recognizable form. Textile designs
demonstrate the variety of ways this form was de-
ployed: a hammer and sickle could appear as a
visually prominent motif or somewhat camou-
flaged in an allover geometric pattern. Yet a
drawing by an unidentified artist of hammers in-
terwoven with gears (p. 32), a perfectly accept-
able symbol of Soviet industry, was rejected by
the Artistic Council for no clear reason.

The most prevalent themes in textile designs of the period declare the priorities of the
Communist leadership under Stalin: industrialization, transportation, electrification, youth,
agriculture and collectivization, and sports and
hobbies, all of which would help to create the

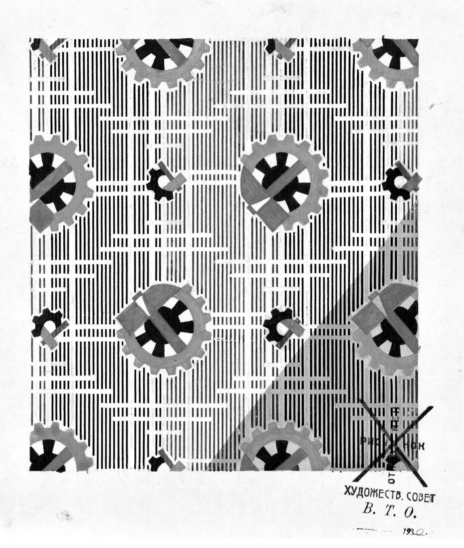

Hammers and gears, 1930

Designed for Trekhgornaya Manufacturing

Watercolor on paper

21.6 × 21 cm (8½ × 8¼ in.)

ideal workers' state. In many cases, however, there was a vast disconnect between the utopian vision reflected in the fabrics and the harsh realities of Soviet life, which was characterized at that time by famines, a severe housing crisis, and mass arrests. This incongruity may partly explain why Soviet consumers were less than enthusiastic about the textiles, decidedly rejecting their thematic designs.

INDUSTRIALIZATION

In 1929, Joseph Stalin and his economic planners announced the first Five-Year Plan. The stated goal was nothing less than to transform the primarily agrarian Soviet Union into an industrialized country within five years. Although factories and industry had occupied a central place in the earliest Soviet visual propaganda, it was during the first Five-Year Plan that industry became a national obsession bordering on hysteria. Factories operated twenty-four hours a day, seven days a week, and workers who exceeded the unrealistically high production norms were awarded "Hero of Labor" medals and certain privileges, such as higher pay and access to better housing. Although it fell short of the proclaimed goals, the first Five-Year Plan more than doubled Soviet production in heavy industry, including the production of steel. Moreover, the plan was completed in 1933, one year ahead of schedule, realizing the popular slogan "Five in four," which conveyed the hope that the targets would be reached faster than planned.

Textile design reflected the national focus on industrial production. For example, a 1930 design by Sergei Burylin depicted the exterior of a factory, its activity signaled by a smokestack blowing smoke. Although the artist included recognizable architectural forms, he transformed the buildings into an abstract pattern of repeating geometric shapes in alternating colors, thus combining appropriate thematic content with techniques of good graphic design, such as strong vertical and horizontal elements. The factory theme was further abstracted by Raisa Matveeva in a textile featuring stylized industrial motifs. Other common images were gears, belts, rotors, and wheels. In a textile by an unidentified artist (p. 39), such machinery parts traverse the blue ground in elegant lines. Another fabric, designed by Lyubov Silich, communicates the dynamism and speed of a rotor using techniques found in Italian Futurism, including repetition and swirling patterns to convey motion. Human figures rarely appear in these images of industry, so a design sketch (p. 41), by an unidentified artist, of a figure working at a furnace is especially interesting. Textile manufacturing itself is represented in designs depicting weaving, sewing, and spools of thread. Although considered light industry, textile production was seen by the public and the state as necessary and important in the drive toward industrialization.

Industry-themed textiles were part of well-coordinated efforts by the Communist Party to inspire enthusiasm and loyalty in recently urbanized, semi-literate factory workers and, more importantly, to express solidarity with Stalin's countrywide process of industrialization under the first Five-Year Plan. Yet all of the propaganda—posters, clothing, and films—only highlighted the dismal realities of urban life, which was characterized by overcrowded and unhygienic living conditions in barracks and communal apartments, food shortages due to famines and inadequate supply lines, and constant threat of arrest if complaints were made too loudly.

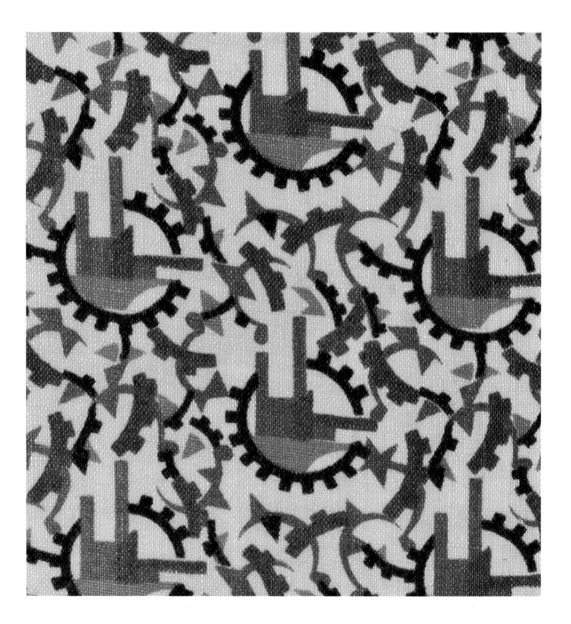

Smokestacks, hammers, and gears, 1929

Raisa Matveeva (born 1906)

Manufactured by Ivanovo-Voznesensk factories

Printed cotton plain weave

10.2 × 8.9 cm (4 × 3½ in.)

OPPOSITE

Belts and gears, 1927–32

Manufactured by Ivanovo-Voznesensk factories

Discharge-printed cotton twill

12.7 × 18.4 cm (5 × 7¼ in.)

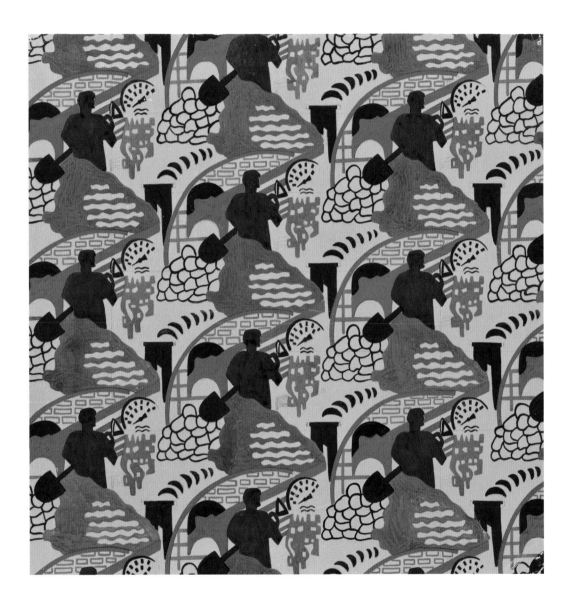

OPPOSITE

Wheels in motion, 1922–30

Lyubov Nikolaevna Silich (1906–1992)

Manufactured by Ivanovo-Voznesensk factories

Printed cotton plain weave

36.2 × 26 cm (14¼ × 10¼ in.)

Factory workers, 1928–32

Watercolor on paper

29.5 × 29.2 cm (11⅝ × 11½ in.)

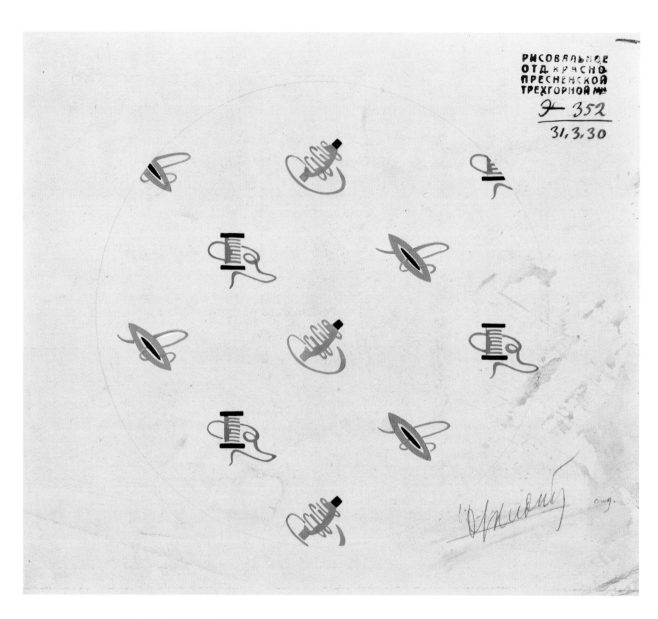

Spools and bobbins, 1930

Designed for Trekhgornaya Manufacturing

Watercolor on paper

31.8 × 36.2 cm (12½ × 14¼ in.)

Fabric and rollers, 1930

Designed for Trekhgornaya Manufacturing

Watercolor on paper

48.3 × 44.5 cm (19 × 17½ in.)

TRANSPORTATION

As part of their quest to transform and modernize the Russian landscape, Communist Party officials embraced the airplane and commissioned the party to bring aviation into daily life. Textile designers' preoccupation with airplanes corresponded to countrywide efforts to raise public consciousness about aviation through the organization of events and lectures, the publication of literature related to aviation, and the creation of local clubs and reading circles devoted to aeronautical subjects. The rigid, geometric airplanes on one textile (p. 49) contrast dramatically with the dynamism and implied motion of another artist's propeller design (p. 48), and Zinaida Markina's airplanes mingle effortlessly with birds in a teeming sky. Yet all of these designs were meant to acquaint the Soviet population with the field of aeronautics and to stand as a symbol of Soviet technological superiority. One anonymous drawing (p. 51) typifies the urban utopia, complete with airplanes, factories, and cranes, that Soviet propagandists predicted.

45

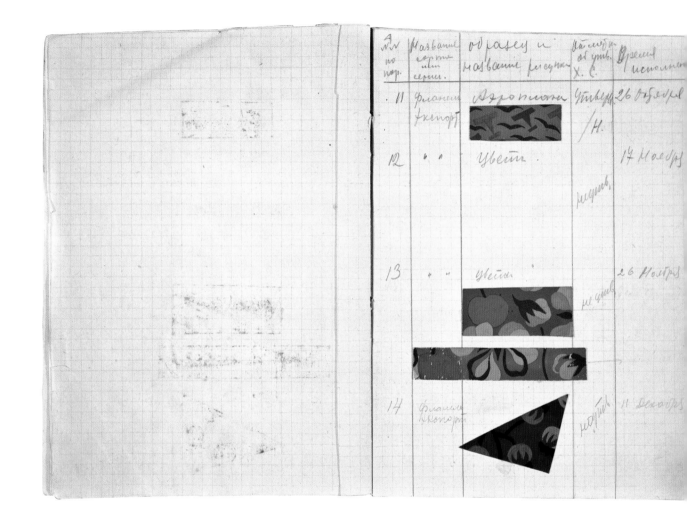

Designer's notebook of textile designs, 1930–31

Zinaida Markina

Notebook page with pasted watercolor-on-paper samples

20.3 × 15.2 cm (8 × 6 in.)

Locomotives and train motifs are also common in textile designs of this period. As early as 1919, trains figured prominently in Soviet propaganda because they played a key role in the transportation of raw materials from rural areas to factories. In that year, Leon Trotsky—one of Lenin's close colleagues in the Bolshevik Party

Birds and planes, early 1930s

Zinaida Markina

Manufactured by Krasnaya Paika

Printed cotton flannel

14 × 17.8 cm (5½ × 7 in.)

and commander of the Red Army during the civil war—called for an entire propaganda campaign devoted to trains in order to motivate the populace to work in train depots and repair the badly damaged locomotives. This campaign included posters featuring trains, such as the Nikolai Kogut poster illustrated on page 16, and plays about trains to be performed in train stations. Given the important role of trains in industrialization, it follows that railroad motifs would be a suitable theme for textile design. As the examples on the following pages show, even a decade after Trotsky's campaign, trains still had an important role in Soviet visual culture.

Propellers, 1928–32
Probably manufactured by Ivanovo-Voznesensk factories
Discharge-printed cotton plain weave
18.4 × 11.7 cm (7¼ × 4⅝ in.)

OPPOSITE
Airplanes, about 1927
Tatiana Chachkiani or Raisa Matveeva (born 1906)
Possibly manufactured by Ivanovo-Voznesensk factories
Printed cotton plain weave
40.6 × 22.9 cm (16 × 9 in.)

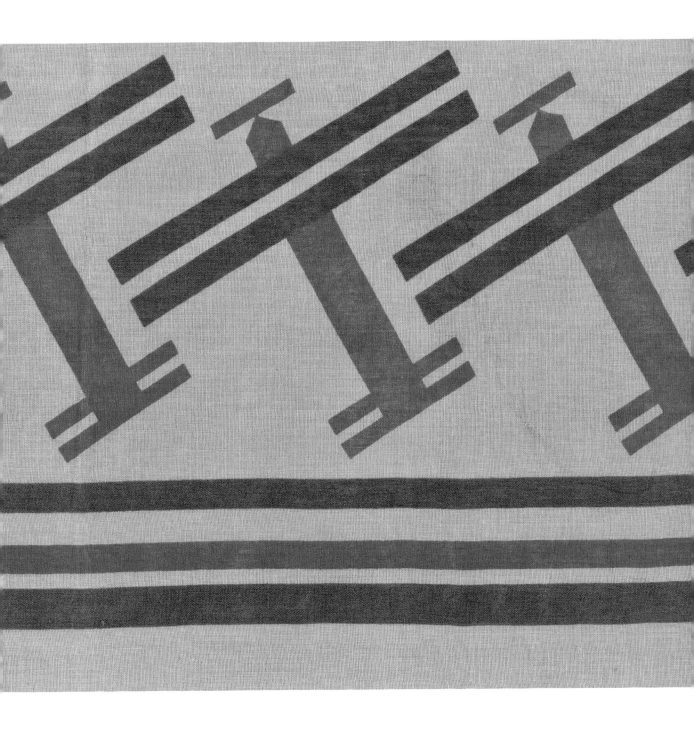

Trains, tracks, and signals, 1928–30

Manufactured by First Factory of Printed Cotton

Discharge-printed cotton twill

14 × 16.5 cm (5½ × 6½ in.)

Factories and planes, 1931

Designed for Trekhgornaya Manufacturing

Watercolor and colored pencil on paper

22.9 × 27.9 cm (9 × 11 in.)

Locomotives in the desert, 1930

Ter Gevodyan

Watercolor on paper

39.4 × 34.9 cm (15½ × 13¾ in.)

C.6.

Locomotives, 1920–30

Sergei Burylin (1876–1942)

Possibly made for Ivanovo-Voznesensk factories

Watercolor on paper

19.7 × 22.2 cm (7¾ × 8¾ in.)

ELECTRIFICATION

Supplying the entire nation with electricity had been at the top of the Communist Party's agenda since 1920. Electrification was touted as the key to transforming the agrarian country into a modern state. This goal was loaded with ideological import, symbolizing Bolshevik aspirations to transform and literally "enlighten" society at all levels. Electricity would unify the vast Soviet Union—composed of Russians, Uzbeks, Ukrainians, and Tatars—and allow peasants across the nation to listen to radio broadcasts of Communist Party speeches and read Soviet newspapers even in the darkest days of the long arctic winter. Lenin's formulation "Communism equals Soviet power plus electrification" became a widely used slogan in poster production; a poster by Gustav Klutsis from 1920 proclaimed "Electrification of the entire country." Some party members showed their enthusiasm for Lenin's electrification program by naming their children Elektrifikatsiya (Electrification) and Ninel (Lenin backwards).

Fig. 5

"Electrification of the entire country," poster by Gustav Klutsis, 1920. © 2006 Estate of Gustav Klutsis / Artists Rights Society (ARS), New York

The bold promises were initially unfulfilled, however, and it was not until 1928 that the necessary resources were devoted to electrification. During the first Five-Year Plan, electricity became a theme once again in the Soviet visual environment. Textile designs incorporated this theme in multiple ways: with literal depictions of light bulbs, or with more abstract images that suggest electric charges and electricity pylons. Even these abstract images would have been easily legible, especially by urban dwellers who had seen many posters over the years featuring the electrification theme. In addition, work had progressed in the electrification of the cities and smaller towns, thus making electrical apparatuses familiar sights to the average Soviet citizen. The electrification campaign was one of the few instances in which the visual propaganda was matched by tangible results.

РИСОВАЛЬНОЕ
ОТД. КРАСНО-
ПРЕСНЕН КОЙ
ТРЕХГОРНОЙ М-

₸°198
28.12.29.

Light bulbs, 1929

Kabykov

Designed for Trekhgornaya Manufacturing

Watercolor on paper: textile border design

31.1 × 36.8 cm (12¼ × 14½ in.)

Waves, 1927–32

Manufactured by Ivanovo-Voznesensk factories

Printed cotton plain weave

17.8 × 13.3 cm (7 × 5¼ in.)

Pylons, 1928–30

Manufactured by Trekhgornaya Manufacturing

Printed cotton plain weave

15.9 × 16.8 cm (6¼ × 6⅝ in.)

YOUTH

The slogan "Under Communism there is only one privileged class—the children" demonstrates the special status children enjoyed in the Soviet Union. As the hope for a bright and radiant future, children in the early Soviet period (1917–32) were employed in propaganda campaigns as symbols of progress and education. Zinaida Belevich's textile design of children at a demonstration captures the excitement of children carrying red banners while being driven around in a truck, a frequent site at state-sponsored celebrations. The design emphasizes the waving flags, underlining the children's eagerness. In other fabrics, figures are transformed into geometric shapes, yet they are still recognizable as children playing and exercising. One example (p. 66) depicts the theme of education, showing students in a classroom learning to read and write and studying geography.

Children's enthusiasm for their homeland could be officially channeled through the Young Pioneer organization, a mass youth movement

Children at a demonstration, 1928–32

Zinaida Belevich

Manufactured by V. Slutskaya Factory or

Sosnev Amalgamated Mills

Printed cotton plain weave

17.8 × 13.3 cm (7 × 5¼ in.)

founded in 1922 for children aged ten to fifteen. By 1926, there were 2 million members and by 1940, 13.9 million. Young Pioneers participated in rallies, sang songs praising Lenin, and even assisted in laborious tasks such as harvesting crops. A textile by Oskar Grjun, one of the preeminent designers of the Soviet period, is devoted to Young Pioneer women wearing the traditional red scarf and uniform of the organization. Grjun both communicates the uniformity of Young Pioneer members and foregrounds the fact that young women played a role equal to that of young men. For another fabric (p. 68), an artist chose to depict only the attributes of Young Pioneer members: the drum, the red scarf, and the bugle. These symbols were so immediately associated with the movement that the artist could omit the figure of the Pioneer and the textile design would still be easily legible. A kaleidoscopic vision of a Pioneer demonstration (p. 69), by an unidentified artist, offers all the essential characteristics of the Young Pioneer movement: the youthful leader as a central figure, the urban setting, and many children in scarves.

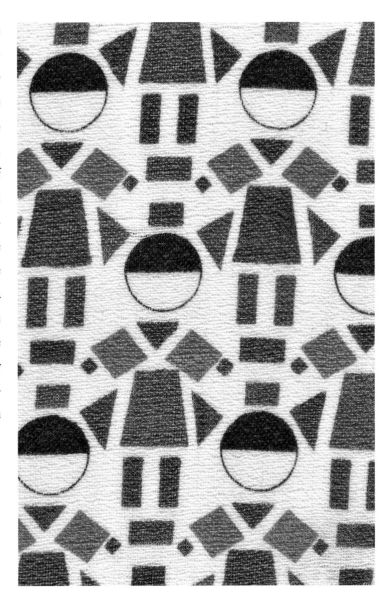

Children, 1928–33

Printed cotton plain weave

14 × 7.3 cm (5½ × 2⅞ in.)

OPPOSITE

Children playing, 1928–30

Elizaveta Nikitina

Manufactured by First Factory of Printed Cotton

Printed cotton plain weave

14 × 11.4 cm (5½ × 4½ in.)

Children exercising, 1930–32

Probably by Elizaveta Nikitina

Manufactured by Second Factory of Printed Cotton

or Trekhgornaya Manufacturing

Printed cotton plain weave

7.6 × 10.8 cm (3 × 4¼ in.)

Education, 1928–33

Printed cotton plain weave

12.1 × 12.7 cm (4¾ × 5 in.)

OPPOSITE

Female Pioneers, 1928–32

Oskar Grjun (1874–1931)

Manufactured by Trekhgornaya Manufacturing

Printed cotton irregular twill

10.5 × 11.1 cm (4⅛ × 4⅜ in.)

OPPOSITE

Young Pioneers' attributes, 1929

Possibly by Bychkov

Manufactured by Trekhgornaya Manufacturing

Discharge-printed cotton twill

12.7 × 8.9 cm (5 × 3½ in.)

Young Pioneers rally, 1928–29

Manufactured by First Factory of Printed Cotton

Printed cotton plain weave

17.8 × 17.1 cm (7 × 6¾ in.)

AGRICULTURE AND COLLECTIVIZATION

The peasantry and agriculture had been frequent themes in Soviet posters and fine art since 1917. Although the peasantry was often hostile to Bolshevik authority and resisted the implementation of reforms from above, agriculture was touted by the Communist Party as the means by which the urban proletariat would be fed and the backbone of the Soviet economy.

In November 1928, the Communist Party forcibly began to turn privately owned farms into collective farms, or *kolkhozy*. Until this time, peasants had been allowed to sell their surpluses on the open market. Collectivization introduced grain requisitioning, and peasants were forced to give up their recently acquired plots of land and sell their produce to the state for a low price set by the government. Peasants retaliated by destroying their surplus crops and killing their animals, resulting in food shortages and even famines. Yet, as textiles of this time demonstrate, peasants were portrayed as willing partners in

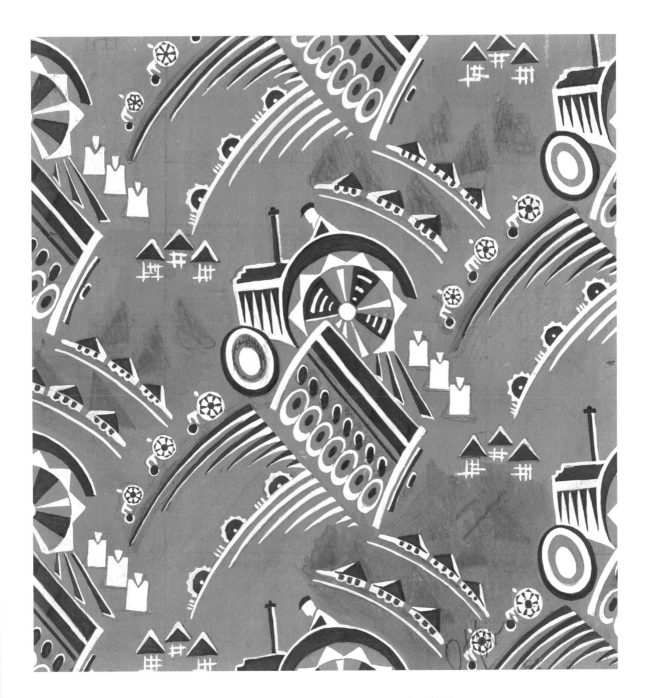

OPPOSITE

Tractors, 1930

Sergei Burylin (1876–1942)

Manufactured by Ivanovo-Voznesensk factories

Printed cotton plain weave

18.4 × 11.4 cm (7¼ × 4½ in.)

Threshers and tractors, about 1930

Watercolor on paper

24.1 × 23.5 cm (9½ × 9¼ in.)

Farm machinery, 1928–31

Possibly by Oskar Grjun (1874–1931)

Designed for Trekhgornaya Manufacturing

Watercolor on paper: textile border design

27.3 × 19.1 cm (10¾ × 7½ in.)

the nation's drive toward industrialization and collectivization.

The government promised—and sometimes delivered—farm equipment, including tractors, threshers, and harvesters, so that collective farms might increase productivity. This mechanization of agriculture theoretically would also free peasants to enter the urban labor force. The tractor, in particular, was a highly charged emblem for the process of collectivization and modernization. It became the symbol of Soviet technological progress in the realm of agriculture, even though as much as 50 percent of farm equipment sat idle and unrepaired at any time. In a textile by Sergei Burylin, a hulking piece of farm machinery is transformed into a sleek combination of simple geometric forms in harmony with the background patterns and images. Some images presented a rather fanciful view of farm life, while others depicted the blurred boundaries between wheat and machine, their interdependence reinforced by the use of similar colors and shapes for both the organic and the industrial.

75

Fig. 6

The Owner of the Land, sketch by S. Gerasimov for town council building in Moscow, 1918

Despite multiple famines that plagued the Soviet republics in the 1920s and 1930s, visual propaganda featured images of abundance in which female peasants can barely hold the resplendent sheaves of wheat. In a watercolor design and a textile by Marya Anufrieva, the peasant women are interspersed with stylized floral motifs, thereby combining the thematic imagery with the more traditional floral designs

77

Women harvesting, 1928–32

Marya Anufrieva (born 1902)

Possibly manufactured by Second Factory of Printed Cotton

Printed cotton plain weave

14 × 19.1 cm (5½ × 7½ in.)

OPPOSITE

Women harvesting, 1928–32

Marya Anufrieva (born 1902)

Watercolor on paper

14.6 × 19.1 cm (5¾ × 7½ in.)

Harvesters, 1928–32

S. Strusevich

Possibly made for Trekhgornaya Manufacturing or

First Factory of Printed Cotton

Watercolor on paper

15.6 × 21.6 cm (6⅛ × 8½ in.)

worn by peasants in prerevolutionary times. A watercolor by S. Strusevich that is reminiscent of folk art, as well as of works by the Russian avant-garde such as Natalja Goncharova's *Hay Cutting*, focuses on abundance through the repetition of figures harvesting wheat. More frequently, these agricultural im-

Fig. 7

Hay Cutting, oil on canvas by Natalja Goncharova (1881–1962), 1910, private collection. © 2006 Artist Rights Society (ARS), New York / ADAGP, Paris

Wheat sheaves and Soviet symbols, 1930

M. M. Shuikina

Designed for Trekhgornaya Manufacturing

Watercolor on paper

27.9 x 32.7 cm (11 x 12 ⅞ in.)

Wheat, 1931

Designed for Trekhgornaya Manufacturing

Ink and watercolor on paper

34.9 × 40.6 cm (13¾ × 16 in.)

SPORTS AND HOBBIES

Physical culture (*fizkul'tura*) was pinpointed by
the Communist Party in 1925 as a way of drawing workers and peasants into social activities.
Although they had initially denounced bourgeois games such as tennis, by the mid- and late
1920s Communist officials recognized that all
forms of sport had both social and physical
value. Consequently, images of sports and ath-
letic hobbies abound in the textiles from this era.
One fabric by an unidentified artist depicts men
running. F. Antonov's wallpaper design featuring soccer players exemplifies the Soviet philos-
ophy of sports in which men of all nations are
equal on the playing field. Furthermore, it corre-
sponds to the official emphasis on team, rather
than individual, games. Other textile designs
show water sports, such as sailing, and winter
sports, such as skiing and ice skating. Like the
textiles themselves, sports were employed as a
method of transforming the individual into the
new Soviet person, with collectivist rather than
individualistic aspirations. Furthermore, these

Sprinting figures, 1928–32

Manufactured by Ivanovo-Voznesensk factories

Printed cotton satin

15.2 × 18.4 cm (6 × 7¼ in.)

OPPOSITE

Soccer players, 1929

F. Antonov

Ink on paper: wallpaper sample

49.5 × 49.5 cm (19½ × 19½ in.)

sports-themed designs promoted a vision of Soviet daily life that incorporated leisure activities. With the end of the first Five-Year Plan, and the corresponding normalization of workers' schedules, leisure activities became an option for the first time under Soviet rule.

Sailboats, 1928–33

Printed cotton plain weave

8.9 × 7 cm (3½ × 2¾ in.)

Sailboats, 1928–33

Printed cotton plain weave

18.4 × 13.3 cm (7¼ × 5¼ in.)

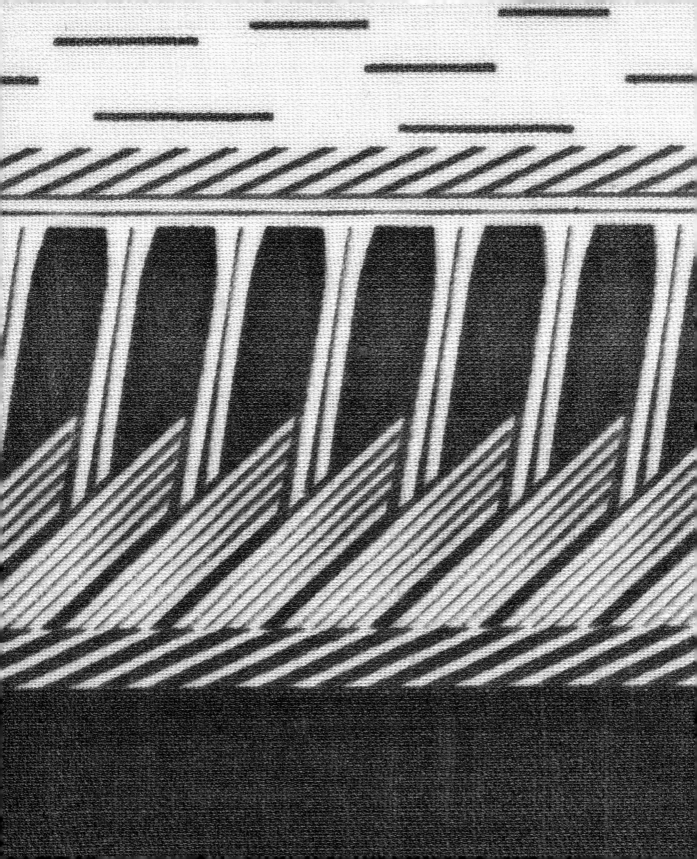

THE END OF THEMATIC DESIGN

On December 18, 1933, the Council of People's Commissars, the Soviet equivalent of the United States' White House Cabinet, published a resolution titled *Inadmissability of the Goods Produced by a Number of Fabric Enterprises Using Poor and Inappropriate Designs*, thus putting an end to thematic textile design. There were two primary reasons for this proclamation: one, the infighting about appropriate designs and subjects for fabrics actually slowed down textile manufacturing and the distribution of desperately needed clothing to the nation's citizens; and two, the citizens generally refused to buy or wear these propagandistic garments and household fabrics. While Soviet citizens may have tolerated the hyperbolic messages they encountered in posters, literature, and films about Soviet progress, perhaps hydroelectric dams on their pillowcases was too much to bear.

The demise of thematic textile design coincided with a more general phenomenon in 1933 and 1934: the acknowledgment of the

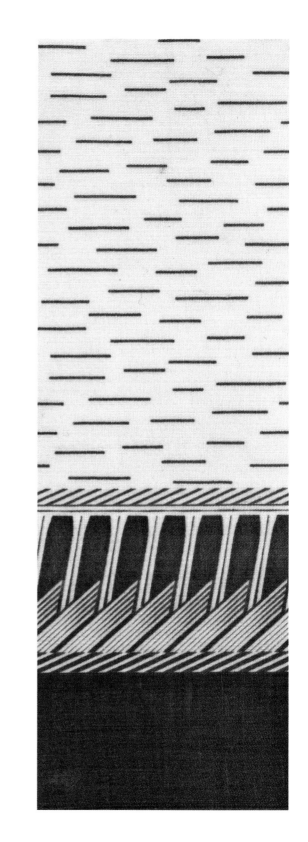

Soviet citizen as consumer, and a retreat from the radical asceticism associated with the first Five-Year Plan. With the inauguration of the second Five-Year Plan in 1933, Soviet economic planners took into account the new Soviet person not only as a worker but as a consumer of goods, even luxury goods. In contrast to the first Five-Year Plan, the new plan aimed to manufacture more products for the household, and home décor became a widely discussed topic. Because thematic motifs were effectively banned, textile designers returned to designs based on floral and geometric patterns. Nevertheless, despite the fact that the thematic-design experiment had been short-lived and rather extreme, the surviving textiles illustrate that thematic content and good design were not mutually exclusive, since many of the textiles are beautiful objects as well as historical documents.

Fig. 8

Floral textile by an unidentified artist, late 1930s

OPPOSITE

Hydroelectric dam, about 1929

Manufactured by First Factory of Printed Cotton

Printed cotton plain weave

17.8 × 7 cm (7 × 2¾ in.)

SUGGESTED READING

Douglas, Charlotte. "Russian Fabric Design,
1928–1932." In *The Great Utopia:
The Russian and Soviet Avant-Garde,
1915–1932*, Solomon R. Guggenheim
Museum exh. cat., 634–48. New York:
Guggenheim Museum, 1992.

Strizhenova, Tatiana. *Soviet Costume and Textiles, 1917–1945*. Paris: Flammarion,1991.

———. "The Soviet Garment Industry in the
1930s." *Journal of Decorative and Propaganda Arts* (Summer 1987): 161–71.

Yasinskaya, I. *Soviet Textile Design of the
Revolutionary Period*. New York: Thames
and Hudson, 1987.

Zaletova, Lidya, et al. *Revolutionary Costume:
Soviet Clothing and Textiles of the 1920s*.
New York: Rizzoli Publications, 1989.

Symbols of industry, 1927–30

Darya Preobrazhenskaya (1908–1972)

Manufactured by Ivanovo-Voznesensk factories

Printed cotton plain weave

17.8 × 9.5 cm (7 × 3¾ in.)